dANGERous bODIES

Sundress Publications

Copyright © stevie redwood
ISBN: 978-1-951979-63-8
Library of Congress: 2024938328
Published by Sundress Publications
www.sundresspublications.com

Book Editor: Tierney Bailey
Managing Editors: Tennison S. Black, Erin Elizabeth Smith
Editorial Assistant: Kanika Lawton
Editorial Interns: Whitney Cooper, Kenli Doss, Hedaya Hasan, Caitlin
Mulqueen, Isabelle Whittall

Colophon: This book is set in Amiri, titles are set in Castellar

Cover Image: Clio Sady
Cover Design: Kristen Ton
Book Design: Tierney Bailey

dANGERous bODiES

stevie redwood

GRACE ROT
BASEMENT MUSEUM

Morning steeps. A cutlass of light splits you
                    from the world.
You want to want it all. You do, only sometimes
you can't live inside it. The world
with its clock-tower theatre,
the world with its light-show streets.
Sometimes a grace museum. Sometimes
the basement rot. Sometimes it's the man
with the bread & the birds
in his palm. Or: it's the welded copper wing.
It's the boy with a winter
beneath his skin & the bare-skinned girl
he buries. The honeybee
& his holy curse, the dying
he does for the hive.
It's the beak in the flower's glory.
The stunted fruit dead on the vine.
It's the scars on your kneecaps & all
the hands clasped. The outstretched arms
of the park bench you perch on
& the people they gatekeep from sleep.
It's the feast in the grocery store
dumpster. The padlocks sealing it shut.
It's Stevie Wonder's *Ordinary Pain*
anointing the radio
while you scribble your name on the rent check.
The neighborhood kids playing
cops & robbers, their red-ringed mouths
a Kool-Aid fusillade.

The one who wears out
her dollar-store guns & a quarter
-century later makes a pretty penny
for each lead round she reddens
in the mouth of a robber.
It's the man spooning mashed bananas
between the tender gums of his six-month-old
                        pocketing his knife
& joining his friends for a Friday night
Proud Boys rally.
Sometimes it's the room
with the light on
& sometimes
the house on fire.
The blaze is the baptism,
sometimes,
& sometimes the requiem.
Maybe you thaw your fingers. Maybe
you swallow the smoke.
& the birth-red clouds are a sacred question,
or else they're the war moving in.

[D[s]CONtentS

~ lIGHT ~

~ WeAtheR ~

~ E A r T h ~

~ METAL ~

~ FIRE ~

~ ATMOspheRE ~

for my co-conspirators—we freaks & menaces; antagonists & beasts

I have love in me the likes of which you can scarcely imagine
and rage the likes of which you would not believe.
Frankenstein's Monster

Your Body Is a Weapon
The Wombats

The rich are only defeated when running for their lives.
C.L.R. James

LIGHT

∞ (MÖBIUS ENTERS A VACUUM) ∞

(00000)

there is a room you end up in, clench into awhile. it's small & infinite, like a tunnel, & you are both beginning & end, & there is no end, & you do not remember the beginning. it's cold there, maybe. you cannot tell. there are no walls. there is no earth. everything is strange. you know it well.

(0000)

there is a room people go to & shutter in sometimes. it's infinite & small, like a door. some know how they got there & some just wake up there one day. the room is no where. it is here. & there. & here.

(000)

there is a room i shudder into & disappear awhile. i know what happens there, but i always forget. i forget what's happened there & i also know. it's infinite & small. there is no door. i've been there over & over. the room has no memory of me.

(00)

there is a room we clench into awhile. all of us are in it & every one is alone. small. infinite. it's familiarly strange. there is a tunnel. there are no walls. we've been here. & here. & here.

(0)

there is a room. it is here. & there. & here. there is no door. until there's a door. we come back from it or we don't. it's that simple. & that hard. you are both memory & forgetting & there are no walls & there is no beginning & you know it well & everything is strange & you do not remember the waking.

B E R T H

Near-sunrise & a billowing mist. A starboard bulb bursts into stalactites
slicing sharply from the ceiling to our feet, their fellow broken blades
a swift storm's litter on the deck.

> *O, mother: the ferocious, the beastly love of your freightship lost to the night.*
> *O, misguided vessel of quiet cargo. O, windowless cabin. O slow leak.*

The eastern dawn shatters, its yellow slant of light scattered long to the
horizon.

> *I arrive in a tangle of seaweed & coughing up krill. Plankton. Plastic. Pickling bile.*

The skyline, murky—but yonder press. Your guess is our command.

> *The world's oldest melody a gurgle in my lungs. Creature of barnacles. Creature*
> *of bioluminescence. Creature of bottomfeeding. Creature of scales.*

Steer with conviction. Steer with all your might. Throw caution,
wing it forth to the swallows of the weed-black deep.

> *Creature of hybrid. Creature of holes.*

Your flesh like paper in the graying light. Like pooling milk.
Like a skin-taut question held up to the winter sun.

> *O, to beg of the dark-rich silt to feed us. O, to weave of the weather a shield.*
> *To make springlike the coils of a thing night-purple and spreading,*
> *inky tentacles clutched wide to compass the heart.*
> *To make of a splintered craft awry a yawning lush*
> *of sea-bottom, waving bed of bending ease.*

Oh, mother.

O, to buoy on broken boughs adrift.

To open, drink, to gulp the saline sea.

O, to spy, wet-brown,

the lapping tongue of shore.

————————(DISAMBIGUATION)

1. [octopus] arms are joined at their bases by a web of tissue known as the
skirt, at the centre of which lies
the mouth.
(Encyclopædia Britannica / entry: octopus)

2. [t]he [mollusk] radula is a spiked, muscular tongue-like organ with multiple
rows of tiny teeth.
(Wikipedia / entry: octopus)

3. I'm not a girl, not yet a cephalopod.
(disambiguation)

i was born a meaty tangle of arms
just like any other creature of the chasm
any many-suckered salt-covered beast
like every unfathomable animal,
faithful predators we be.

recipe for a ~~girlhood~~:

step 1.

start with all the little deaths.
shake them out into an empty globe sliced off
at the equator. let them trample each other
for the peak of the trap heap like crawfish
snapping in their harvest pail.
them desperate. them brutes.
them boneless. them grasping,
like they aren't already dead.

we the predators. we the prey.
we the spineless. yes, no
backs to break. be broken.
we the shapeshifters.
we the soft-bodied, ready
to [shr]ink.

step 2.

winnow the water. measure the salt.

we the cyanide-blooded.
we the reaped.

mercy. mercy.
i want out of this harvest. you too. take your armor off
my mouth. take my arm. we can ladder out of here
arm over tailfin. claw over arm. i'll be the sucker
this time. just promise you won't leave me
stuck. tuck in your scythes. arm my mouth. i want out—

we the abyssal
the hadal
the Hadean.

step 3.

trap the reapers.
crack the bones
of the deathly
into threes.

sinews shirr my limbs into a skirt.
at the center of my skirt is a mouth.
in the gully of my mouth
is a sawtooth tongue.

step 4.

grind the bones
against my tongue-teeth
one by one
by one

1986 BLEW UP THE COLUMBIA SPACE SHUTTLE & THE CHERNOBYL NUCLEAR POWER PLANT & US SOCIAL SUPPORT PROGRAMS & MEANWHILE I LEARNED ABOUT LOVE

watching plain Cheerios wither in a soup of tap water
when we'd drained the milk carton thickly into our growing pains.
Orange juice with pulp when we were lucky. From *not it!*-ing
over who'd get pancaked into the middle backseat
of the '85 Sable (me—forever me).
From clambering onto the countertop
to filch forbidden candy. From wheedling for live goldfish
at the annual fair of the neighborhood private school
none of us attended. From naming our goldfish *Goldie*,
as no child has ever done before. From keeping it alive
through six years, two moves, three rentals,
& a floor-flopping 6.9 Richter event.
From repurposing bathwater
as bathwater, with a wink
from family-of-five water bills.
From puckered cans of Chunky soup
straight from the cupboard
to our afternoon bellies.
From KFC buckets & biscuits
muddled with gravy if we were good.
Dim sum if we were celebrating.
From always choking
on my Chinese name.
From being folded like dumplings
into our bedclothes, moon after moon,
crooning our farewell ditty
to a litany of the mundane: *Goodnight dinner.*

Goodnight Goldie. Goodnight castle.
Goodnight goodnight goodnight.
I learned love along highway marathons out of town,
seatbelted in the wagon's backward-facing row,
playing sweet & sour with drivers
stewing in their traffic-scowls.
From comedy after comedy sketched
into our book of Mad Libs.
From crayons neglected on the car seat
& melted eternal into the upholstery.
I learned love from my father's childhood
dreams of priesthood & the habits
he stepped out of. From the whispers
of my confessional phase.
In the churchpews of backtalk rebellion.
From my penance pose in the stairway corner.
On genuflect, arms out like angel wings—
no. Out like a crucifix.
I learned love by the throttled light
-house of my mother's gusty shame.
From straight-C report cards
& vending machine lunches:
hot cheetos & a long slug of milk.
I learned love along the great elastic horizon
between low-slung Dickies & high-slung boxer shorts.
From crop tops, Chuck Taylors, & eyeliner thick
as pubescent longing. From the abracadabra of crush
from a person to an unbearable ego death.
From the vortex of acne & hormones & the body
puppeteered. Adolescent insomnia & adrenaline jolts.
From the well of my earliest whiskey swig
& the virgin kiss it birthed. From tongues
tripping over mushrooms & the time they were shiitake.
In the chain-link refuge of the chainsmoking alley
behind the high school I dropped out of.
Between visits to the shrink.
At the sacred altar of the night

front stoop & its starry ash
of Parliament Lights & fall-cold cheeks
& the reek of teenage captivity.
In the selfhoods we talked each other into.
From surviving our mothers, mostly,
together. From being too much,
too much,
much too much.
From underneath
our skin. From seeded
through our gums.
From tethered to an anvil.
& how my anger fell
like stormlight across a room.
& how i was
& was not
forgiven.

DEAR BABY

dear baby,

how does your heart break? since you don't have words, do you think in
feelings? in senses? in absences, in the language of want? do you think in
vignettes of longing, or is it not so romantic as all that? here i go again
confusing survival with desire. i don't know how to do this. i wish i
could swallow my words, dissolve them in acid, erase all the evidence.
vestigial sounds curling from my throat like smoke, hot sibilance, a
thrash of hissing, small bolts of glottal, the ghostly percussion of an
ancient cadence of need. without words to choke on, perhaps there would
be room to let the light in: to open, photosynthesize, satiate absence with
a different end of the world.

dear baby,

i'm sorry i told you that everyone hates you. not because it isn't true,
but because i failed to tell you that you don't deserve it. people hate you
because you haven't yet learned how to lie.

dear baby,

how does something become possible? how does anything become? how
is it that you exist, crying, breathing, blinking, new, knowing nothing,
now, of the bothers to come, to become, to make you less possible? we
become so much less possible. this wasn't always the case, i know.
everything has become. so small. so small, your body, impossible, yet here
you babble, bubbling over with need, with nothing, not knowing of the
impossibilities to come. so small, your bothers, but they're everything.
you know. the smallness of your knowing is different from ours. you
know. you know.

dear baby,

i lied before. i love you. i always will.

dear baby,

there are so many things i want you to teach me. there are so many
things you still know how to do. i wish i could tell you you'll get to my
age & remember to wonder why. that you'll still know how to sleep when
you need to, that you'll eat when you're hungry, that you'll scream when
you need help. that you'll poop and wail and smile and study everything.
that you'll let yourself be held. that you'll yell just to learn the sounds you
make. that you'll cry for love without shame. i wish i could tell you that
you will still gape at that leaf, and that fly, and that shadow, and that
speck, and that nothing, and that glance of light, and anything that
moves or doesn't, and the miracle of your own finger. i wish i could.

WEATHER

i wake to a man singing glory unhinged   his windpipes a trembling galestorm   the traveling
brume   blossoming   an inkblot overhead   *how strange*   i think in pictures   *to find this*
handheld ease   with the unlikely tempest of my dreams   our fingers a flesh-fold   filigree to
mime our latticed veins   a pine tree slicing soundly up the sky   snaking its name between my
eyes   & i wake again to my own buzzing   breath rattling sinus walls   a richter 6.9 & a
saturnine crawl   through kaleidoscope gauze &   a gossamer of thunderous shake   into
a cold   & golden morning & a grasping   for the hem of the threadbare real   & later
when i dawdle under a bedsheet   of leaf & cone above tire-tracked mud   & puddling wet my
hands full with the raveling   echo of wanting of   weight   there is the pine   but instead
of treeing its pitch   in the breeze it is   toppled in thick slices   round wedges ringed with
age   ringed like saturn   ringed like wed   like woven fingers   veins a braid of dendrites
loosed to strands   & scattered red

& don't you see the man unhinged   was never singing   he was always a buzzsaw
rough-toothed & throat-sharp   wingbeats a gurgle serrating his hum   & the dream was
never a dream the tempest   was never a song the breathing   was never easy   but a bundle
of thread-knots   axonal & harsh   & listen—

[& WHEN THE FOREST IS LEVELED, IF THE SAW WAILS THE LOUDEST SOUND: HALLOW THE TREES & GO AFTER THE BLADE]

RUPTURE DENTATA

incisive windbite of autumn / a burst-ripe thirst for novelty / an
unfamiliar town & its handwave / of permission / a wet monsoon of
strangers / taut thrust / of bedrock against my ribs / new small-town
friends with their hearts blown wide / a growth-green invitation / *he's
so nice* / chimed the townhearts / *i'll come* / hollowed my mouth / the
ruby-throat birds with their warbling / anticipation on the dying gasp of
day / the shaky pedal / over a night-bridge / to an unlit island of
orchards / the toll inside my chest / the rickety pickup / my bike
teetering in the truck bed / a question mark in the driver's seat / the duo
of townhearts sardined in the rear / their faces / new moons in the dark
/ the car & its quiet chatter / our throats & their rising hum / a flock of
wheels writing snarls into earth / the orchards / a cipher / my
torso / a stone / slowing / arriving / unsticking / the front door / waking
the bulb / a shock of fluorescence rendering our faces / the hearts with
their moons / beaming newer than ever / the small talk / the dinner /
the question mark / unspooling sentences knot by knot / his wolf-eyes
knifing the light / the hungry blade turning / my gut / into a chorus of
warning / the walk we stumbled into / the night becoming / a door /
the question mark keying the lock / into an aperture / the opportunist
storming the hatch / his face a gash / of death-white / his pupils a yoke
of black holes / the moon & its toothless grimace / the opportunist with
his mouth hinged wide / the sour rot / of preying / on too many sweet
things / three moons hemorrhaging light on the gravel / a stout bottle
ready to shatter / my stone fist clamped to its belly / poised / to open it /
into a mouthful of canines / the opportunist with his jaw full / of wolves
/ & when we say *it could have been worse* / what we mean / *we want not* /
to remember / when we say *we do not* / *remember* / we mean *only the birds* /
thrumming their song / at the long gravelled ore / of our throats

MESSAGE FROM A CARGO SHIP

naked casing of human, deserted
& rucked along wet pacific shore
spotted by two waxen torsos with
legs to stroll through fog & eyes to
eagle emptied skin :: they toed
jumble of body like dead thing
it was :: pitiful :: featureless ::
pockets for eyes & no mouth to speak
of :: mined for its sinews :: no matter ::
no mind :: fleshsuit leathered by weather
or water :: fingers weathered by water
or work :: girdled with seaweed ::
engraved with the teethmarks
of beasts :: sucking life
from the overboard :: arms :: ribs ::
breast :: salt :: meat :: torsos
with legs kicked yellow thigh of
hollow human-shaped bag
until shin folded over mouth &
foot hid forehead :: torsos with
eyes shrugged shoulders & legged
down cold coast shore

HABITUATE

you sprawl across the thistle of a weedy slope,
bones splayed over the hill-belly,
friends beyond your fingertips.
fog between your teeth.
you watch a scant coyote
feebling along the flank.
too much rib,
less feral than winter.
pluto yoking at the sun. light out
of reach. this will become another day
you don't want to remember.
it's lucky you're wired
for forgetting. your housekeys,
the trash you didn't take out,
gas stove still lit.
the way it smelled right before burning.
the people you've lost. been.
the ease of loving
more than you fear.
that one night.
that other one.
those blank many years. your friends
capture the coyote in the crosshairs
of their cameras & you pluck dandelion
after dandelion from the dirt.
on the ridge-hip, the coyote stills.
her knees are brittle, giving,
failing. too many hands
have tendered her.
too many humans have rendered her
tame. habituated,

she belongs to no one,
belongs to everyone
before herself.
she looks familiar. she looks like someone
you forgot. she looks your way
& you look around,
eyes dilated, reflecting
dandelion manes. you twist one off at the neck
& raise it to your lips. blow. watch the plume
shatter into fragments of a fortune.
the scatter of a wish. *don't tell anyone,*
your friend warns, *or it won't come true.*
you know this is a false story
& say nothing. you've learned keeping quiet
makes other people's wishes truer,
that things held below the tongue
are the slowest seething pill.
the coyote opens her mouth,
her throat, perfectly hollow & void
of howl. she has forgotten how to make something
out of breathing. she tries. again. again,
percussing into the wind. toneless,
beautiful as rubble. wretched as dust.

REVENGE   FANTASY

in the dream
i find out
from a stranger:
your heart stopped,
painless, more merciful than you
given the brutality you
so casually inflicted, how
in relationship
with the best of us
you promised just enough
enough—
our trust in
everyone
suddenly gone,
a ransacked house in
a ghost town

you're dead &
in the bluntest way,
without warning
& regrettably it was
deserved,
so nonchalantly &
guilelessly violent your idea of being
was; how you did
your very worst
to make us crazy,
to make us lose
everything,
our best selves
emptied like
a winter desert
on an ugly planet

BATTLE | GROUND

& for the wolf-whistlers, the cat-callers, the people
-eaters; the take-aim-&-masturbate
-ors; the take-what-I-want-ers; the what-do-you-mean
-NO-ers; the get-inside-your-head-under-your-skin
-into-your-blood-&-lymph-ers—I thought I'd have so many
fuck yous to cough up from under all that ash.
Instead I have quicksand. The face of a bottom
-feeder. Flashlight for a mouth. Eyes that are dead
-end tunnels, never widening, never tapering, forever
open as closed, empty & full
of wind.

i.
The first time someone fucked themself next to me
I was on the busiest bus line in the city, & too young & naïve
to believe it. When I tell you I thought they must have been
stroking some pet they'd smuggled onto the coach
& not petting the stroker
they'd woken & choked, I'm dead
serious. *Perhaps it's a ferret,*
I lied to myself, & believed it.
When I tell you I knew just enough
to be scared—I mean I already knew
what I'm expected to sacrifice
myself to protect, so I stayed put & fixed my face
into the shape of a half-hinged door.
When I tell you I stayed,
I mean I played—nice, along,
dead. When I tell you I worried
first for the smuggler, I only mean
I was doing what I was told.

ii.

The next time someone fucked themself next to me
without asking, it wasn't *next to*
so much as *against*. I was too young & naïve to tell
the whole truth, & I still don't
call it an act of war. Instead I lie
down now & again & hold my own arms
loaded against my chest, spinning out
of the world with its gravity, reaching
for the sound of falling
water. I'm told it's always storming
somewhere, & believe it.

iii.

The first time I fucked someone who asked
what do you like &
is this okay, I was
too far flung & aggrieved
to know the answers
might one day come.
When I tell you I said
I'd say *no* if I didn't want
to be touched, I mean
I held the truth locked
next to my chest.
& when I say
next to, I mean again
against. I mean I lied to myself
& believed it.

iv.

The first time someone fucked themself next to me
because I wanted it, I asked
do you want to & wondered
if their *yes*
was a whole truth.
When I tell you I asked

do you want to, I only mean
ten times. When I say ten times,
I mean *not nearly enough*. When I say
enough—

v.
The first time I fucked someone
who held their own hands
into a cup & made a little home
for me to sputter truths into—
who said *yes, please* &
no, not right now—
asked *what do you need*
& *what don't you want—*
I stretched for the sound
of falling water,
& we held our own hands
open to our chests,
& when I say I clasped a true thing
next to me, this time
I mean *close,*
mean *almost—*

& when I tell you
I fell, I mean back
into gravity,
& when I tell you I fell,
I mean like the rain,
& when I tell you I fell,
I mean into my body,
& when I tell you
I fell—
I mean
out of love
with the war.

EArTh

GREENER LOVERS

The maidenhair ferns were greener last September, when I was here in the cold
red autumn caretaking our little potted garden; while you tended
to your warm white lover across the world—but I know how you love
your private morning ritual, your tryst with the plants & the windows
& the graying dawn & the backyard cats still furled on the roof
of the slumbering neighbors; how you rise in your haze, set the tea kettle
growling, fill the watering can with last night's pasta water,
push a thumb gently into the soil of each soft plant, & I like to imagine
how you might sing them & yourself out of sleep: throat open, sun-up,
spout down, petrichor, morning hair, morning voice, still raspy, underwater-
ing, but fertile with care, so when I notice the leaves more crêpe paper
than chlorophyll I leave them be, watch the color unthreading
from this lobe & that, & when another whole frond has gone withered
& pale, I bend tenderly until the break, always at the knee, small bone
spiking brittle from its ganglion of roots, where I leave it to yield until
tomorrow, or maybe next week, when it's safer to pluck without killing
whatever new green there is growing—

ODE TO SPITTING IN YR MOUTH

february now & it feels like summer / all heat-bloat / no rain / i go to the ocean to cool / & the shore / has become an insatiable drunk / the ocean waves / but i don't / know its face so drawn / so shrunk so i shrug / & walk / & i walk & the water / slides farther & farther away / i unweight / my boots / their anvil of sand / refill them my cold granite feet / back home / in a vortex of bedsheets / you weep as tho to replenish the sea / to level / the drought / i spit in your mouth / to barter the ocean / its emptiness / for my want / i deluge & come / on my knees / await the unremarkable death / of the earth / & still thirsty / the evening opens / its mouth / one block over / our neighbor jimmy lives in a tent / by the condo construction / when i wake / to his howls curdling the air / i fill your mouth / with my fingers / as if they could busy / every wailing tongue / you fill me with forgetting / drown / his moans with mine / & in the dark we pull each other's hair / say *i'm a lez for you* / & mean *abolish the family* / say *make me bleed* / & mean *healthcare should be free* / you paint my skin with angry red / slap-prints when i tell you to / remind me / i know / how to hurt myself better / than anyone / it works / until the sun clocks back in / for an eleven-hour shift / for which she like us / does not get paid enough / to keep her from setting every day / things on fire / just to keep the floorboards warm / in the kitchen / you turn up / the oven / say *talk dirty to me* / i unsheathe / the meat knife / my breath at your throat / whisper / the blade to your hip / trace dreams of the blood / we could tease / from our landlords / run / as tho rivers / could turn / into banks / we save / every drop & sell it for souls / theirs wanting / ours empty / & thirsty / still / thirsty still / thirsty i spit / & i spit & i / downpour

—& i

       empty

             i

                 come

                     on my knees

ODE TO THE HOUSE OF WEEPING QUEERS: #1

we trade notes about loving each other & killing capitalism—

flicked under bedroom doorways, left on the hallway mirror, taped

to the coffee grinder. sprawled across the butcher block m found

propped against a telephone pole on bougie-street trash day

before they hauled it home & got the gristle out. they sanded & polished it

until it was slick & manicured as jeff bezos's idle hands, & less stained

with the blood of other creatures. until it was well-oiled,

gleaming like teeth, so clean we could have eaten

the rich right off it. until one day we did,

& found out they don't taste like chicken after all. we knifed the rich

into mouth-sized bites & ate with tiny silver spoons

k stole from the minimalist housewares store that got a whole building

full of seniors evicted. we chewed & chewed, hungry for a heart

-y cut, but m said when they sliced behind the breast

there was nothing there. we gorged ourselves anyway & bickered

about whether we were still vegetarians. m said yes,

that things only count as meat if they were alive once. k said no,

but it was worth it.

... with each reform, revolution became more remote [...]
But if one were forced for the sake of clarity to
define [*fascism*] *in a word simple enough*
for all to understand, that word would be 'reform.'
GEORGE JACKSON

YOU WALK YR NEW BOOTS
HOME FROM PAYLESS

thru a fenced-off plot of mud   things are suspicious
when they've never been dirtied   like how
fileting strawberries on yr favorite cutting board
corrupts each slice with garlic   but you do it   anyway
you've learned you can't control most things
but at least some you can predict   in this way
you learn to like yr berries better   progressively
perverted   not because they've become good
for you but bc you know   what to expect & in what way
is this not like liberalism? most things are predictable
if you listen long enough   you can hear the earth
rolling over   thru a rolled-up twenty   cupped against yr ear
each dollar a prophet   w/ different fortunes   for you   & me
& the CEO   diamond-studded whiskey glittering
down her chin   as we bathe our cheeks in what's left of the sun
block & walk   outside for ten minutes btwn work
& work to take our paychecks to the bank   & listen
to the birds laughing from their richly papered trees   *cheep*
   cheep   find it sweet instead of gruesome   listen   we learn
to love   what we've been given & how
is this not like exploitation? i want to be careful
not to blame the terribly fucked over & also   be careful
what you learn   to live with   pain   rent checks   presidents
a collection of single socks   broken teeth   no heat

mold on the ceiling   the myth of crime   more violent
than punishment   "countries"   the electoral college
forty hours a week   & cops   & war   & war
&   war &   war   (did you expect that prophet
wd have this many echoes?)   buying water   the unhoused woman
cleansing herself with a bottle next to the curb   the man looking down
from his dirtless $3-million 3-bathroom loft   before calling her in
for an evening   in handcuffs   having nowhere
          to wipe off her dirt

IF I TELL YOU THERE
IS MORE LUST

in violence than lust
in lust will you still think
me a good person—
i'll try again
is it more or less brutal
to want to die
slowly—pain is a kink
like any other
guarantee
superfluously ordinary
sometimes anaesthetic
sometimes excruciating
ask me how i know
meanwhile my entrails are quiet
ly cannibalizing themselves
& how about you would you like to
tell me about your pain
its lust or its violence how loudly
it proselytizes about the end
of the world but what does pain
know about the end
of anything really see pain
is prosaic like any other
violence there is only
a beginning following
an earlier beginning & a be
fore the last time & the time
before that see life closes
& opens with violence but don't think
that means pain starts or ends
there or that the middle isn't

violence too—stay with me
if i tell you somewhere
a politician is lying
asleep among corpses
if i say somewhere
a cop is using
his baton to beat
off if i tell you a CEO
is somewhere sucking
the white from every bone
will you still think *we*
should turn the other cheek this
libidinal violence that closes
& opens people
s lives is ever more
brutal & is it cannibalism
if you're no longer the same
species & anyway look—
this is war

HUNGER | STRIKE

The day the US State dissolves   the US State

of Emergency   it's raining   bureaucracy

& coroner's reports   2407 people   dead last week

from the virus   which   is over says everyone   & the forecast shouts

it's rain! it's rain! more! rain!   a multicultural parade

of protesters   haunts   the Alameda courthouse   melting

pot   of advocates   for people   without jobs

one   a diabetic refusing to eat   sits surrounded

with handmade signs   *Hunger Strike Until Die!*

&   *PLEASE HELP VICTIMS OF GOVERNMENT ABUSE!*

the abuse   being an arrest   of the right

of *mom & pop* landlords   like him   to evict people

from the homes they live in   & do not own

where can tenant live   *without housing*

providers   another sign says   *Tenant and landlord*

are not enemy each other   yet   another he made

after trying   to sue "his" tenants   a parent & child

for non-payment   of rent & failing   18 separate times

so tired   of no longer being able   to feed

his mom & pop family   from the hustle   of another family's labor

in the newspaper   he invokes the Dream   he & America shook hands on

when he arrived   in the Land of Opportunist-y   capitalists call the eviction moratorium   *draconian*

after the Greek legislator   known for consolidating power

in the hands of landowners   against the poor   & I believe

that's what's called   a *self-own*

it's   a dog-eat-dog kinda life   it's   kill

or fight back   it's   feast   or go hungry

& everyone's hungry   only some

eat their own   *Hunger*

Strike   Until Die!

Hunger   Strike

Until   Die!

Do you think

he'll follow

through

FLEURS POETICA
W/ BAD SEEDS

So write
about love
if you want to
the wedding song
the newlyweds dancing
to the beat of The Police
Sting crooning his beloved
stalker anthem

> *Every Breath You Take*
> I'll be surveilling you

& write about love
the wedding banquet
its whole roast pig
the apple in its jaws
or write about flowers
the wedding bouquet
how you caught it
between incisors
whetting against its thorns

Yes, write
about flowers
about plucking the arrangement
petal by petal
picking them off
seed by bad seed
& when you do
ask not *she loves me*
she loves me
not—but a more romantic

interrogation
a more aspirational wedding song—

>   *which pig gets cooked*
>   *(the loudest squealer)*
>
>   *what hog gets caught*
>   *(the greediest liar)*
>
>   *this narc gets hooked*
>   *(the biggest dealer)*
>
>   *that cop gets shot—*
>   *(swine-faced vampire)*

Of course
I'm being unserious,
bad seed implies
the existence of

            bad flower,

                        bad fruit

when we could be talking
rotted tree,
invasive root
So right—
about apple trees,

any *good seed*
in the apple orchard
will kill
the average flower
as in sweetness
flowing
petal by petal
only when they die

METAl

CITY OF SPIES

I'd like to be invisible. Lampshade-headed, chameleonic, a shadow
in the nighttime. Microscope needed. Cousin Itt. Instead I'm a cameo
on a camera roll on an airplane back to who knows where, mid-sneeze
between the shivering tourists & the fog they'd swear to God
contains the Golden Gate Bridge—& God would know, ever watchful
from the towering holy haven of His lighthouse; from the filmy
gated pearl of Her panopticon—& I'm bull's-eye on the Target
CCTV, glowering at the man checking me out at the checkout
counter, me checked out, him oblivious to the strangers' code
for introverts. Yes, I'm captive, black & white in 20/20 lenses
stationed on the 1900 block of Bentham, pointed & shooting me
smashing doorbell Rings. The walls have eyes & photographic
memories—& I'm caught on a reel like a lucky guppy: wriggling
in the open, baited for sport, released at least this time. & I'd like
to be underexposed. I'd like to be a nightmare strip, all ghost.
The negatives of dreaming. An absence in a stolen record.
The long erasure; the empty file; the ruined palimpsest.
A whisper in a windstorm; the wind inside the cave.
& I'd like to be the phantom bridge. I'd like to be the fog.
I'd be lying if I said I never wished to die
face-first.

DOGSHIT

It's Saturday & I'm weary of other people.
Even so, I leave home to find my friend T,
who keeps me up on the neighborhood gossip
& always has her lashes done right.
T lives in a tent among tents
along Hampshire & is dying
for a kitchen to cook in again.
I'll invite you over, she'd said.
You can bring whoever you want.
She needs help getting cat food,
more cash, more warm clothes,
a cell phone, her birth certificate,
& far, far away from her boyfriend.

I pass by the house of the tiny old woman
who isn't friendly & is usually talking.
Hers is the trellis where last spring,
every blister-purple morning glory
trumpeted its dawn to the neighborhood bees;
where leafy hearts camouflaged a sprawl
of knob-kneed katydids in various stages
of living & dying. They're born small & shiny
& greenly bald; balled up & flightless.
Wings grow in their own seasons,
budding with neighboring ginkgo trees.

Last year the old woman caught me
nosing at antennae,
eyeing mandible after mandible
munching her front-yard foliage
into an abstract lattice of light.

She ground her palms.
If you see them, she rumbled,
Crush them—& I did
nothing of the sort,
though I could have—

This spring at the old woman's garden,
the glorious thicket has thinned, its flowers
& leaves leaving, & climbing the fence
instead is a warning: PROTECTED
BY XFINITY HOME SECURITY.
I surveil the meager hedge for traces
of survival against odds: a chewed-up leaf,
a rogue antenna, a trail of tiny pellets,
a nascent wing. If they're alive,
they're burying the evidence.

A block farther from home, a row
of new condos. A poodle-beige
coffee shop haunts the skeleton
of rent-controlled apartments past.
The pavement still boasts
its usual abundance of dogshit.
Face of a sharp-boned realtor
plastered on a sandwich board.
VANGUARD PROPERTIES. 3 MILLION DOLLARS.
2 BEDROOMS. 2 BATHROOMS.
A 2-CAR GARAGE + a picket fence

of teeth. Bleach-white. All caps.
Real estate speculation will pay
your every dental bill. No matter
how many. No matter how much.
A whole new mouth if yours has gone rotten
from filth. One can digest only so much
death—but anyone can wipe themselves clean
if they hustle enough

out of other people. Some theft
is called *stealing*; some stealing:
success. For the right face,
work ethic. Smart bet.
Two degrees? It's not *murder*,
it's *good business*; *good hustle*;
good investment; *good job*—dogshit

still there on the sidewalk after a day.
So is the hubcap. The microwave.
The mustard packets, the campaign mailers,
the swivel chair, the puke. But on Hampshire,
the tents with our neighbors living inside
have been stolen. No welcome mats,
no water jugs, no tarps, no snacks,
no rescue kittens, no more signs
of life. No altar, no mercy. No T.
We promised to clean up the neighborhood,
announces the mayor from doorknob flyers
littering the sidewalk, *and we're succeeding.*

Success. Scrubbed. Swiped. Swept. Homes
aren't homes until money says yes. People
aren't people unless they can work.
The Department of Public Works works
for money. *Work ethic. Good job. Success.*
Well done. One person's trash, another one's
shelter. One woman's shelter,
another's political campaign.

We promised to clean up
the neighborhood,
and we're—

dogshit.
If you see them,
comes the echo,

Crush them—
hands grinding,
teeth glinting,
eyes bright
& knife-sharp—
so keen
to cleanse life
from her doorstep

IT'S ANOTHER SUNDAY MORNING

& I shudder out of chaos into chaos, exiting a dream of sprinting full-speed out of danger into a curt & urgent knocking at the door, & I wrestle free from a knot of stress-gnarled bedclothes, shoot straight from horizontal to standing, nude as a newborn, vision lidded & bleared, fingers grasping for a robe, the knocking now louder & louder & I'm imagining my lover growing fearful on the stoop, sleep-crusted, no keys, mean wind slamming the door locked behind them, bed-nested hair & naked feet a magnet for suspicion, as in neighbor-eyes narrowed, as in *NO SHOES NO SERVICE*, as in clutched pearls & purses, as in *SUSPICIOUS ACTIVITY WILL BE REPORTED TO THE POLICE* & I hear it again now, this grim slaught of knocking, heavy massacre of the front door, the shattering knuckle-rap that means "URGENT! OPEN UP" & still imagining my lover vulnerable, I'm finally there & as I sweep aside the curtain barely draping the glass, the knocking knock-knocks again, this time unmistakable: it's the blows cops are taught will put suspects on edge, & while categorically wrong they're damn right about that, & there's no mistake now but the one I make spinning away from the snarl of the gun-carrying pig who believes he's a man, & I drop the frail curtain as though it's a bomb, like it would kill me if I kept holding it open like that, or as though it's a shield—if I cannot see him then he never saw me—& I flee from the danger, forgetting hunters will chase, & I run for my lover, who is, yes, barefoot, as I am, & on my side of the door, & yes, eyes have been narrowed & suspicious activity has been reported to the police, & I run, & on top of the rapid-fire knocking, the badged gunman's yelling "COME TALK TO ME," my cold feet assaulting the floorboards, "COME TALK TO ME," cacophony calling to chaos, "COME TALK TO ME" & I exit again into danger, "OPEN UP" as I wrench the door wide & his mouth's foamed with rage & I'm lucky it's only his muzzle that's spitting

TRASH DAY TRIPTYCH
OF THE MATERIAL

i.
Monday, headache, coffee, work.
Unholy screech of a trash truck
backing up down the street,
unholy vision of tire tracks
branding the oil-stained concrete
of the colonial abstract,
truck tires rupturing arteries
of the modern metropole.
I open the window, light
an American Spirit,
watch flames burn the paper
red, then black, then white
as ash. I used to smoke only
in the dark. Now I smoke whenever
the church bell rings
or doesn't.

ii.
Monday. I wake up
as ever, run over
by the trash truck wailing
hydraulic exhaust
ion outside my window.
I exhale over the resonance,
startle a house finch
out of the topiary.
The trash collector looks
like my father. I look
toward downtown,
the Salesforce Tower

a parody of itself. The bells
of St. Peter's chime
their brutal measurements
over our lives. Our time, our value,
their rules. I light a Lucky Strike
& count American flags
against the skyline.

iii.
Monday.
I wake up sweating with rage
over wage labor.
Outside, a trash truck beeps
like it needs something.
I'm already throwing everything
I have into the garbage
patch. I want to hurl
my body down
but I won't
do that to a worker. I wonder
what his name is,
how much he gets paid,
if he's disabled yet.
I watch trash bin after trash bin
flip upside-down, shaken
until empty as it gets.
I light the last Parliament
so I can burn something
as I fantasize
about a different
dissolution

TUESDAY BLUES

It's not just any Tuesday,
you think, getting ready

to begin your morning stretches,
first reaching for your phone

to compose a brief mass
guilt-trip: *Friends, it's time to earn*

the privilege of yr citizenship! It's ok if you're not
familiar with every candidate on the ballot.

Just remember to vote
Democrat!—& for a moment you wonder

if you should be more discriminating
about who you send it to,

but then you shrug & select
your contact list. It can't hurt

to remind everyone you know
to vote blue—no matter who

sponsored the campaign ads.
No matter who called for more

public school closures. No matter
who did what twenty years ago;

no matter who assaulted whom.
No matter what apartheid. What borders,

what prison spending, what fraud.
What bathroom bills, what surveillance,

what mining, what wars? No matter
who owns stock in Lockheed;

no matter who it will kill. Keep killing—
keep voting blue. No matter

the 3.1 million people the first
Black american Democratic president

deported. Keep reporting
your neighbor for leaving

her kids to play loudly
alone, again, interrupting

your daily yoga practice,
while she works from the home

of people who don't care
for their own children. Children

& Family Services is responsible
for making kids into valuable

property, but you know some good
Evangelicals from your Neighborhood

Watch who'd love the extra
cash—plus the people

who direct the local CFS are all women,
& you know what that means.

The kids are yelling & bouncing
a ball against the refurbished wall

of your two-story house, which
you've fully moved into, finally,

after nine long months of remodeling.
They're getting louder. You're worried

about your cortisol levels,
& also, those poor kids.

You wonder if any of them eat enough.
You've seen their mother

& she always looks tired. Skinny.
She seems not to like you,

never says hello. You wonder if she's ashamed,
or maybe she just doesn't speak much

English. If she's not home
after you finish meditating, maybe you'll call

the police. You don't like the ones
who are violent, but you've made friends

with a few cops who are good
acupuncture clients. Your favorite

is a lieutenant who just retired
to help raise a beautiful child

she & her lawyer wife adopted
from Korea. She shows you photos:

Sophie smiling on her first day of preschool,
Sophie sleeping next to Hillary,

their toothy golden retriever;
Sophie waving from the police float

at the Pride Parade in a sequined t-shirt:
Love Conquers All.

Your phone chimes with message alerts
as you take your last deep breath

& open your eyes, look around
at the room you've so lovingly adorned:

pale peach walls, a milky orchid,
framed color portraits of naked women

in various stages of pregnancy. You rise
to the strident music of the ball's echoing thud

syncopating the phone's eager treble
& the children's tonal yells, & now

the beagle across the street begins howling
as a siren Dopplers by—which reminds you,

as you lift your cell phone from the corner
of the loveseat, that no one is protected

or served when the bell isn't rung.
You begin to dial, thumb moving

toward *call*; the other hand
reaching up to the window to shut

out the clamor, & then WHAM—
you're grasping more air

than you're breathing, body hunched,
the wind & your phone knocked out of you,

the bouncing noise now
inside your apartment, hard bright ball

quickening its flat blue stutter
along the hardwood floor.

The kids' nervous chatter hails down
around you, shattering against floorboards

next to the shards of your phone's dark
fissured face, into which you now look,

still breathless, & find the dim sputtering blue
of your fractal reflection

buzzing in the static, making you think
god,

I could be anybody—

FIRE

What time is it on the clock of the world?
GRACE LEE BOGGS

IT'S SAN FRANCISCO SUMMER

solstice in the third year of the plague & I'm trying
not to ruminate on death. The heat has lifted

the ambient temperature in the winter
of Mark Twain's displeasure to the climate of a human

fist: a fist of rage; a fist of roses; the fist erected
in solidarity or demand. Clench of a cellular heart;

uppercut to the fascist; the sticky fist of lust. Each one
all the way inside me. Baptized with blood. Ninety-eight

degrees of extinction. The sun won't slide off
this side of the globe until 8:35, after dinner,

& tomorrow the days will get shorter, maybe
fewer, light abandoning its latitude

of questions to seep into the pavement,
wasted. I'll be trying not to think about dying,

about money. The killing that's made
in the business of despair. Today is still

the same temperature outside as inside
my body, & my brain can't tell itself

apart from anything: the shriveled hillside; the displaced
palm tree; the flattened pigeon without its head.

The sky that will not open. The dust that hasn't settled
from the construction workers building

the profit profile of the neighborhood
house over home, block upon block, bone by bone

by bone. By graveyard. By cinders. Bye-bye.
Ash of the rent-stable apartments

the landlord burned down for insurance
against his own incineration, lit by the strike

his tenants come together, now apart. Scattered
to the of gales of relocation, caprices

of public housing stock. I can't tell myself apart
from the ruins. From the wind. From the clocks we wind

our lives to. I can't tell myself a part
of the fable of time without hearing my own

morals rattling like slow change
in the vacuum of my bank account. Bank

breaking. Back breaking. Backs broken. Been
broke. Humpty Dumpty was a tyrant. The king's men

wouldn't have troubled themselves for a peasant,
& we would never have fallen

from such great heights. Trickle-down
nothing. Kick down walls. When they go high, we go

under. Underground. Undermining.
Dig deep. Dig deeper. My fist

rabbled open. The rubble dusted up.
We're trying not to despair about the dying

& trying not to kill from the despair
& trying to make a passage to tomorrow,

keep from falling off the face
of the clock.

THE BUTTERFLY EFFECT

It opens with a loudmouthed silence.

The sky agape in homograph,

a hole in the shape of a wing.

Kindergarteners roadrunner home

on training bikes,

bellowing into the calm.

Into their yawning traps flies

barren air, a tongueless breeze,

a swarm of phantom bugs.

Along the eerie street people gut the paneled pavement,
roll out florid welcome mats, dirt carpets sown thick with red
mountain balm   baby blue eyes   purple coneflower   goldenrod.
A roll call of native blooms to court their tiny neighbors. A cup of sugar
water in the birdseed, spill of honey in the soil.

The ricochet of birdsong caged

deep inside their memory, hungering

for the hum of sails to carry it along the wind.

Months drawl on. The silence lengthens, grows.
The streetfront gardens begin to wilt, their pollen thinning
for want of probing tongues. Honeybees feeble through singly,
guzzle themselves numb. They stumble home to lonely nests dead
drunk with the nectar of a neglected garden they slurped up
by themselves. The neighborhood children hardly know them:
to thank them for their labor; to fear them for their sting.

From behind the kitchen

windowpane no longer frenzied

by a mesh of spidersilk, by a fever of fire-

thirsty moths—the woman waits

for the timer to call her children in

for dinner, gazes on the sallow poppies

closing to the dwindling day, dreams

the bee that might alight on one

tomorrow if she's lucky. She stares out

without seeing, vexes the salad

greens with a wayward thumb.

Rations them leaf by leaf as though

the earth is running out. Out

-side, the horizon swallows

the sun and she watches

her children disappear inside

the graying light. She looks and dreams

the swallowtail knee-deep in petal sugar

as though everything depends on it,

she looks and dreams and looks

and dreams and hears

the timer ring.

IN FRISCO THREE DAYS AFTER THE IPCC REPORT DOES NOT SAY *TOO LATE*

Bernal Hill hits eighty-five degrees

When the doves begin to settle
I untuck my legs & leave my roost
to trundle upslope, watch
the loudest light go down

It's strange what you hear up here
& what you don't
Not the quiet implosion
of the woman
under the buckeye
dirtying her shins
but a bolt of laughter
hurled from half a mile below

The heat's long sigh, relieved
as the sky slides
a wrinkled nightgown
over its silvering dome
Sirens wailing their emergencies
back & forth
The groundhog underfoot
rearranging its paws
for sleep
not the neighborhood dogs whistling
but the insomniac crows
gossiping
about their days
the weather
their thoughts

on climate change
On the freeway everyone hurries
as fast as they can
toward the rest
of their lives
their bodies shed beneath them
like shadows under pressure
of a midday sun
briefer than the light
that cast them

Strange that in its years
the moon's never seen
its own phases, strange
we can look
everyone in the eye
but ourselves
& the sun
doesn't know
its own light

Along the map
lines run
all through bodies
of land & water
spilling shadows
on the earth beneath them
like saplings under pressure
of a waning sun
longer than the struggles
that grew them

& calling this climate
change
is like calling this violence
a *country*
what lies here
we're told

to fold into
Calling this global
warming is like calling
the electrician
when the stove sparks
the whole house aflame
another fire
we believe
we'll outlive—
one more blaze
we won't look
in the eye

Everyone's hurtling
toward tomorrow
forgetting
forever
isn't a place
we can visit
for awhile

FIRE ENGINES

I've been listening to the rain whisper
through my sleep machine for months
of skin-dry winter, when we thirst most
for refuge & other bodies. Seasons no longer
divide themselves predictably into the year.
Fall overwinters into a sluggish spring. Summer's
drought-cracked face saran-wrapped onto telephone poles
broadcasts an august reward.
Fire season erupts onto the landscape
six weeks premature, fishhooked by tempest
& overgrowth. Here's California painting
an impression of itself, bleary & bled out
onto the canvas like a frigid sweat. Burned-out tree trunks
stippling the earth's soiled leather like a six o'clock shadow.
Too late, too long. Too soon gone.
The ground thirsts for respite & water
bodies, desiccated & desperate
to burn. & we haven't yet got to the heat
of the matter—which is, as ever,
people are dying who could be saved.
Or: people aren't dying so much as being
extinguished. Snuffed out. Too soon. Too gone.
Fire season rampages far too long, fanned by generations
of negligence & genocidal engines. Fire
fighters, long culled from cages, ambushed
& felled by many contagions: a lung-hungry virus.
A death-hungry violence. The warfare of property.
By the time of the spread: too few hands left
to dig out the fire lines. Too many holocausts
at once. Here's America performing
its theatres of siege: infernal, so hungry

to extinguish its people & light
every match.

ATMOspheRE

ANY MOMENT

Yesterday I bounced a tiny bird
off the windshield of a borrowed car
that may never before have struck warm flesh
I sped up the hill   swept salt from eye   to sleeve
did not pull over   In my quaking lap
a glass box bloomed red with pulseless scallops
leaking fortune from their wounds   A wild bird
gets a ditch in lieu of a burial   & in the wrong moment
any thing is a weapon

We walk all day   all days   clutching clumsily in hairsplit hands
cubes of thin glass   each containing a chaos   of grotesque pink scallops
the raw twitching hearts of every live thing we see
A long day's work to keep them   any wayward moment
to lay down their pulse   Any moment   a tremor
any moment   a knife   & we wear whatever armor we can cull
[leather headphones shoegaze   vigilance   switchblade   caution snarl]
& know at any errant moment   the facade may shear clean off
eucalyptus bark skinned naked in a sharp rogue wind our mortality bare
or did you imagine a life   less easily cleaved

I look up   to see my callow heart
behind a smudge   on the hand-box
of a man across the street   Back down
to feet my gaze catches   in its light
the glint   of a thin glass knee   glass
thigh   glass hipbone

& if looking forward
to the future   isn't
the ultimate suspension

of disbelief—

go ahead
& shatter

the whole thing

DEMI ◗ NOVA

in the spectacular
mundanity
of dying
like everything else
stars plummet
unsuspecting
thru the everyday
infinity
of absence

some people think
the looking is romantic
i prefer to study
what is clearly dead
kaleidoscopic longing
for an end i recognize—

if nothing else
i want to choose
my own demise

DELIVERANCE

It's been 2021 longer than anyone
can remember   & Portland is 112 degrees
California's dry as a desert throat
& likelier to asphyxiate   heat waves catch
like a virus   birth funeral after funeral
at the lip of Lake Tahoe   where it's never been hotter
a goggle-eyed tourist films a mama bear
trundling her triptych of cubs
through the threat   of a swimsuited crowd
muscling down the people-peppered beach
into the water's tepid respite
out of the ambient heat
the video goes viral
some headlines fawn   *ISN'T IT CUTE?*
others   *WE ARE ALL FUCKED*
my headline blinks   *IT'S BOTH*
I watch on a screen in the kitchen
sip coffee   like it's any old day
separate the garbage from the compost
as tho three fewer peach pits in the landfill
might patch the ozone layer   Jeff Bezos rides a phallus
-shaped machine   from Texas to the stratosphere
to prove there is nowhere   he won't pillage
we turn our clocks to 11:11
wish on every star   for his safe return
to the plutonian depths that forged him

11 minutes pass & disappoint us
he returns instead to earth
thanks the workers
whose lifeblood he extracts

for fun & money

In those 11 minutes
    like any other 11 minutes
            he has blinked 220 times
                worked 0 seconds
                    & become $2,451,900 richer
I said
    two million
            four hundred fifty-one thousand
            nine hundred dollars richer
In those 11 minutes
    amazon delivery workers
        have deposited packages
            on 102,262 doorsteps
                & made $3.30-$4.58 each
In those 11 minutes
    hospital delivery workers
        have helped 2,941 new people
            tunnel out of other people
              & into the global population
                  which traded those 2,941 new people
                      for 1,166   newly dead people
                              including
                65 people murdered
            by intellectual property laws
        vaccine imperialism
      medical apartheid
    & reopening for business as usual
      1,166 newly dead people
        including people
            who died on the job
                people who died bc
                    they could not find a job
                    & people who died
                      from job-related stress & illness
            1,166 newly dead people

                        including
                  countless unhoused people
               whose lives counted
            whose deaths will be
         neither counted
      nor accounted for
In those 11 minutes
      fast food workers have made their orders
            known   all over the so-called US
                  striking & rallying   for $15 an hour
                        before taxes   earmarked for all
                              manner of warfare   meanwhile
                              Jeff Bezos has gotten two million
                                    four hundred fifty-one thousand
                                          nine hundred dollars richer

In those 11 minutes
            7 women   spent
               a long 660 seconds   of the second
                  of three long days   in Wadena county jail
                     bc when they put their bodies on the Line 3
                        pipeline destruction site   they threatened
                              the dominance of property   capital
                                 & heteropatriarchal settler colonial relations
In those 11 minutes
            some people lived
                              every second
                                    as tho
                                          the end
were ~~not nearer,~~
                  ~~& nearer,~~
               ~~& nearer,~~
            ~~&nearer,~~
               ~~&nearer~~
                  ~~&nearer~~
            ~~&nearer~~
               ~~&nearer~~
                  ~~&nearer~~
                     ~~&nearer~~

                              inevitable

COMBUSTIBLE MATTER

"[The] US military is a bigger polluter than as many as 140 countries...
[&] remains the single largest institutional consumer of hydrocarbons in the world."
theconversation.com, 2019

On a hazy Monday morning, the sky sheds a nearby city cinder by cinder.
In this soot mote, the bark of a brittle tree that passed the wildfire
to another; in that particle, vestige of a child's plastic
fire truck. Inside, I seal the windows to keep the smoke
out of my mouth, already hot with other ashes. The kitchen stifles,
ruptured with heat. Under a glass vase on the table, the newspaper
lists pandemic deaths like today's stocks, laments another unnamed
teenage boy inside a classroom with a gun. Weighting the pages,
a single sunflower withering blade by mustard blade

                                  becomes a rumor.

The elementary school next door shakes off the wind-pilled sheet
of a brief, cruel summer: heat-ripe with children, ringing
like a drill. It's recess time, & no one's on the playground
but the thick spectres of carbon monoxide & seismic wrath. The wraiths
of futures past. The kids yell from cooped inside,
with & without masks on, trading cards; snacks;
dangerous air. One hazard for another. Lung damage
for lung damage. A recess roulette. Sweaty with bottled desperation;
thirsty & throttled with all they're now forced to escape

                                     & imagine—

In a short half-century, those among them still alive
in their fifties will have moved higher & higher up along
with the sea level; watched the ocean's magnificent swell
fold shore upon shore forever into its mouth.

Or it's like this: in a quarter century, when they're in their thirties,
they'll remember the indulgence of the bittersweet marriage
of coffee & chocolate, from back before drought
drove the prices of both beyond the ceiling;
drove fields of both dead into the ground;
buried whole towns of farmers alive.

Or it's like this: in ten years, when they're teens,
they'll have seen monarch butterflies migrate en masse
into history books, next to red-legged frogs, gray whales,
blue herons, redwood forests, axolotls, 49% of all insect species,
San Francisco, Guangzhou, Mumbai, Santo Domingo,
Kiribati, Tonga, New Orleans, Micronesia, Bangladesh,
& half the human population.

Or it's like this: in ten days from now, when they're
ten days older, they will be ten days closer
to the end of their lives, which will be decades shorter
than the lives they'd dreamed of, & we'll be ten days
deeper into denial, & the earth will be ten days nearer
to being one degree too hot to inhabit.

It's like this:
in ten shallow breaths from now,
or
in ten
seconds
from now
this second
we could all be
deciding to build
a global movement
of workers against war
& militarism; of militant anti-
nonviolent solidarity against mass
production & shipment of hydrocarbon-
fueled weapons; of Raytheon antagonizers &

Exxon saboteurs & people who do their childcare
& others who cook their food & squatters who make up
extra beds & fighters who teach group shield tactics & healers
who share their medicines & medics who facilitate skillshares &
people willing to struggle & sacrifice & die & live for each other
& elementary school children who remind us how & why to dream & yell
& make & scheme & laugh against the war; to sing & fight & cry & make
up & dance & question & tell the truth & play for all our lives; to love like
it's what will save us—

REVOLUTIONARY LETTER #1312

after Diane di Prima
for Wendy Trevino

Toward every world you want to make & unmake:
ask yourself what you are willing to do
& not do. To have & not have. What you would give,
could take, would risk & protect, would birth & nurture
& kill. Find others who know that the war is not coming,
but here. Find those who are ready to sacrifice
what they love. Find people who already have.
Find people who'll tell you what they know
& what they don't. Study with people who are still curious.
People too tired to be curious, but who fight & fight
& fight some more. Care for them like your kids'
futures depend on it. Find healers & bring them in.
Ignore people who say that that isn't important.
Learn who to trust & when & how much. Find people
who have fucked up & people who've changed.
Find people motivated by rage & people
motivated by love & people who understand
these are often the same. Find artists who care
about what art cannot do. Learn what you love
& do well & can offer: chauffeuring or witness
or sign-making or a couch or meal delivery
or money or security or Narcan or grief ritual
or medic skills or propaganda or song or legal support
or de-arrest training or banner rigging or strategy
or snacks or meeting space or cleanup or or or or
Find elders & youth who will listen
to each other. Find people who will fight
for the truth. Be willing to be the messenger

even when it makes a bull's-eye of your mouth.
Know that people will try hard to kill
what you're doing & don't let them
get in the way. Find people who know
that it's always been urgent
& people who move fast & people who move slow
& people who understand the stakes

YOU TELL ME YOU DON'T WANT THIS LIFE

but do you

& i know

the same ache

its acrid thickness

making a bomb

of your throat

in the winter

of my bedroom

i hibernate

imagine

going out

instead i perch

inside

the clutter

on the ceiling

there are many ways

of leaving

a woman rushes

into the passenger seat

of her own car

shovels noodles

down her throat

as tho she's being timed

a couple minutes over

her boss

is counting down

do you know

a synonym for *unravel*

is *ravel*

is all

the falling

apart

do you know

the way

back

together

do you know *i*

& *you*

are interchangeable

in the thesaurus

as on the timeclock

did you know

we mean

the same thing

somewhere

on mission street

a flutter

of pigeons

squabbles over bread

torn apart

& scattered

by the man

from the panadería

who wears a mask

all day at work

when he goes home

to feed his parakeet

he forgets to take it off

do you know

another synonym

for *you*

& *i*

is *alone*

did you know

if *you* or *i*

is *alone*

long enough

we begin

to lose

our meaning

meaning

there are many ways

to leave

weed is a word

we give life

we never asked for

a thing we resent

for how it refuses

to die

that is you

& i

resent the impulse

to live

in spite

in spite

there's a knot

of sourgrass

in the dirt where

i buried my mouth

its silent grave

a homonym

for any undesirable thing

& there are many

leavings—

somewhere

in the winter

of my throat

under a snowdrift

a bomb

lies

& readies

GRATITUDE

Thank you to the following magazines & journals, who took a generous leap of faith in publishing iterations of these poems:

bedfellows magazine, "ODE TO SPITTING IN YR MOUTH"
Elderly Mag, "THE BUTTERFLY EFFECT"
Midnight Sun Magazine, "COMBUSTIBLE MATTER"; "GRACE ROT BASEMENT MUSEUM"
Prolit Mag, "DELIVERANCE"; "YOU TELL ME YOU DON'T WANT THIS LIFE"
Protean, "FIRE ENGINES"; "Trash Day Triptych of the Material"
Stone of Madness Press, "(disambiguation)"
Tripwire, "IT'S SAN FRANCISCO SUMMER"; "Revolutionary Letter #1312"
Underblong, "ode to the house of weeping queers: #1"
Vagabond City Lit, "HABITUATE"
Wax Nine, "MESSAGE FROM A CARGO SHIP"; "YOU WALK YR NEW BOOTS HOME FROM PAYLESS"

ACKNOWLEDGMENTS

my thanks to the people in the following places who saw fit to publish
some of my weird poems: *Stone of Madness Press, Flypaper Lit,
Vagabond City Lit, Underblong, Protean Mag, Prolit Mag, Midnight Sun
Mag, KCET, Wax Nine Journal, Elderly Mag, bedfellows mag,* & *Tripwire.*

deep gratitude to Leila Easa & the brilliant writers & people in her CCSF
poetry class in the spring of 2019. to Ross Gay & the incredible cohort
in his workshop at the Juniper Summer Writing Institute: i fuckin lucked
out! to sacha & fancyland—i am forever & ever in your debt. to Megan &
Rick Prelinger: thank you for the infinite sanctuary of the Prelinger
Library. to Angel Dominguez: thank you for offering me such generosity,
faith, & confidence in such a vulnerable moment—& ever since. & to
everyone at Sundress—especially Tierney, Tenni, & Erin, who have been
encouraging & flexible & kind during every single step—thank you for
making this easy!

to my family of origin, most of whom i fervently hope never read this
book: i'm thankful. it's complicated. i love you.

Val, i love you ferociously & always will. what more is there to say?
Eva: you have been a beacon, a wonder, a tether thru many hurricanes i
thought for sure would take me. Aby, you are & have been, since the
moment we met, the very sunshine of my life. Sabrina: words could
never do it. to the moon & back & beyond with you, always. Andi, your
generosity & kindness & brilliance are a true boon for the world. may we
always, always, always do the monster mash together. Kate, my fellow
water-bearing overthinker: if for no other reason, i'll be grateful to
Tw*tter for putting us in orbit together. thank you for trying so hard,
always, to do right by your people. Wendy: what a gift to know you. i

have learned so much from you. your care & brilliance & commitment are astounding. Clio—co-conspirator of co-conspirators—i write madness for & with you. Angie, arlo, Bri, Eleanor, Elisa, Joni, karyn, Melissa, Muffy, Nora, Raia, scout—thank you for your friendship; for learning & growing together with me.

to m: shotgun princess; dyke of all trades; encyclopedia of song lyrics; sweet beautiful freak; barista antifascista; forever punk; babe of gay babes doing the labor behind the labor behind the labor; lionheart lover of the people—thank you for being in it with me; i'm so lucky to be in it with you. you deserve every beautiful thing.

to everyone i have ever considered family, or ever will—it's a trip. we're doing our best, i think. thank you for how hard you've tried. keep going, if you can.

& to every body, past present & future, made dangerous by force or by violence; by necessity or by will: stay. ready. the war is already here—& there, & there, & there. the least we can do is fight.

we make each other possible. we make possibility emerge. & there is so much more to do. may our love & our fury destroy & remake it all.

sOURcES

"I have love in me the likes of which you can scarcely imagine and rage
the likes of which you would not believe" is from Mary Shelley's
Frankenstein: The Modern Prometheus.

Combustible Matter's epigraph derives from an article from
The Conversation, find the article here:
  https://theconversation.com/us-military-is-a-bigger-polluter-than-as-
  many-as-140-countries-shrinking-this-war-machine-is-a-must-119269

ABOUT THE AUTHOR

STEVIE REDWOOD is a disabled toisanese jewish neuroinsurgent introvert homotrash littledreamer bigmouth bitch living & dying in frisco. they're unimpressed by scene queers, artifice, & pacifism. they're fond of shittalk, porchsitting, leaflitter, & riffraff. they dream a different end of the world.

OTHER SUNDRESS TITLES

www.ingramcontent.com/pod-product-compliance
Lightning Source LLC
Chambersburg PA
CBHW031143090426
42738CB00008B/1195